MW01489385

for Youth

CONCORDIA PUBLISHING HOUSE · SAINT LOUIS

Copyright © 2022 Concordia Publishing House
3558 S. Jefferson Avenue, St. Louis, MO 63118-3968
1-800-325-3040 • cph.org

All rights reserved. No part of this publication may be reproduced, stored in a retrieval system, or transmitted, in any form or by any means, electronic, mechanical, photocopying, recording, or otherwise, without the prior written permission of Concordia Publishing House.

Scripture quotations are from the ESV® Bible (The Holy Bible, English Standard Version®), copyright © 2001 by Crossway, a publishing ministry of Good News Publishers. Used by permission. All rights reserved.

Illustrated by Anthony VanArsdale

Manufactured in the United States of America

1 2 3 4 5 6 7 8 9 10   31 30 29 28 27 26 25 24 23 22

Table of Contents

God Creates All Creatures

Read Genesis 1; 2:10–14. When God created Adam and Eve, they were perfect. He placed them in paradise—the beautiful Garden of Eden. Watered by four rivers, it was a lush, beautiful home filled with flowers and trees covered in delicious fruit.

When they disobeyed God and ate the forbidden fruit, they deserved to suffer a life of misery, loss, and sorrow followed by never-ending pain and suffering in hell. Instead, God loved them and chose to save them. He promised a Savior who would crush the serpent's (Satan's) head and free us from the eternal suffering we deserve by having Jesus take our place and suffer and die on the cross for our sins.

Adam and Eve's sin shattered more than their relationship with God. It poisoned their relationship with each other. Selfishness and distrust filled their hearts as Adam blamed Eve for his sin. Eve now had a sinful desire to run their marriage instead of being an equal companion and helper to Adam.

But one more loss happened with their fall. Adam and Eve lost their rule over the earth. The first way this loss showed itself was a curse that God put on the ground. No longer would the land work the way God had originally designed it to work. Driven out of the Garden of Eden, Adam and Eve had to work hard to grow food from the ground from which the Lord had formed their bodies. Compared to Eden, their new home was like a wilderness. Instead of having abundant food hanging on every tree, they found that the ground grew weeds, thorns, and thistles much more easily than it grew food. Ever since, we have had to fight to control those weeds. If left to themselves, they would spread and choke out and kill our food.

The climate and weather were also affected. Large stretches of land became dry desert and waterless wilderness. Without water, families couldn't thrive. Other areas suffered a drought as the rains stopped falling and rivers and lakes dried up, causing extreme shortages of food, also known as famine. Whenever we face a lack of water or drought conditions, we are reminded that our lives are impossible without the mercy of God, our Creator. You'll read more of these experiences in the coming weeks. And you'll also read about God's greatest love when He sent His own dear Son, Jesus Christ, to die and rise again. He did this to assure us of eternal life when He returns to judge all people and restore His shattered creation.

This week, you will take a look at some other Bible passages about water that help us understand how bad our lives are without God.

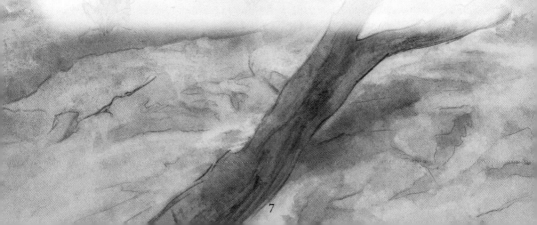

God's Promised Land

READ DEUTERONOMY 11:1–17

When God brought Israel—the nation He raised up from Abraham, Isaac, and Jacob—out of Egypt, He led them through a dry, scary wilderness. Moses described it in Deuteronomy 8:

> [The Lord your God] led you through the great and terrifying wilderness, with its fiery serpents and scorpions and thirsty ground where there was no water, who brought you water out of the flinty rock.
> (DEUTERONOMY 8:15)

Did you notice the phrase "thirsty ground"? Can you picture the deep cracks like open mouths panting for water? There is no way the people of Israel should have survived ten days in the wilderness. But God preserved them and their flocks and herds for forty years! The Lord led them to springs and oases. When there was no water for miles and miles around, He brought them water out of a rock. Read how that is described in Psalm 105: "He opened the rock, and water gushed out; it flowed through the desert like a river" (Psalm 105:41).

Look at what life is like in our world. Isn't it like the wilderness where Israel lived for forty years? It is filled with doubt, insecurity, jealousy, envy, and hatred. People are thirsty to be loved, and accepted, and to have true friends. Where can we find true love and peace? We can look to our family and friends, but the only place we can find true, lasting love is from Jesus Christ. He is the Son of God who came into this wilderness to show us God's love, take our sins away, and give the new life He won for all of us on the cross.

Just as God was with Israel during their forty-year stay in the wilderness, He will be with us all the years we will live in this world. He satisfies our thirst with the people He brings into our lives—especially our brothers and sisters in Christ. But more than anything, He satisfies our spiritual thirst with His precious Word, the water of our Baptism, and the body and blood of our Savior, Jesus Christ, in Holy Communion.

In Deuteronomy, Moses recorded his last goodbye sermons to Israel. As the twelve tribes of Israel camped on the shore of the Jordan River with their backs to the wilderness, Moses pointed across the river to the land God had promised their fathers Abraham, Isaac, and Jacob. Notice how much his description of the Promised Land reminds us of the way he described the well-watered Garden of Eden in Genesis 2:

> But the land that you are going over to possess is a land of hills and valleys, which drinks water by the rain from heaven, a land that the LORD your God cares for. The eyes of the LORD your God are always upon it, from the beginning of the year to the end of the year. And if you will indeed obey my commandments that I command you today, to love the LORD your God, and to serve Him with all your heart and with all your soul, He will give the rain for your land in its season, the early rain and the later rain, that you may gather in your grain and your wine and your oil. And He will give grass in your fields for your livestock, and you shall eat and be full. (DEUTERONOMY 11:11–15)

Remember, it was never God's plan for Israel to live in the wilderness for good. He was leading His people through the wilderness to the Promised Land. It is also not His purpose for us to spend eternity living this life on the cursed earth. He is guiding us through this wilderness to our promised land—the new heavens and the new earth, which Jesus will restore when He returns to raise and make all of us believers perfect forever on Judgment Day. Then we will live in a paradise even better than the Garden of Eden. It is a land "that the LORD our God cares for" (Deuteronomy 11:12), a land in which we will live with Him and have the chance to walk, talk, eat, and drink with Him forever.

Thanksgiving for God's Care

READ PSALM 95

We often hear stories about the terrible damage we are doing to the earth. We hear scary warnings of global climate change, shrinking ice caps, rising temperatures, and great destruction. But the one thing you never hear is what God, our mighty Creator, is doing. Satan is trying to convince us there is no God—that everything came here by chance and we humans are the only ones who can save our planet. Or if you believe in God, the devil is trying to convince you that God doesn't care. He's trying to convince us it is only up to us to save our home.

That is how the people of Israel thought while traveling through the wilderness. They forgot God was with them, protecting them from all harm, giving them water to drink, and providing them manna, which was special food God delivered every morning. They thought they were all alone and complained each time they were thirsty or bored with their lives. They also forgot God was guiding them to the Promised Land, a place where they would never have to worry about being hungry or thirsty again if they trusted God and served Him.

Sometimes, people scare us by making us think we are on our own and it is up to us to take care of ourselves and save our world. But listen again to how Psalm 95 describes our mighty Creator—not just the Creator of this earth and all the life that covers it, but also the uncountable planets, stars, and galaxies that fill the universe.

> The LORD is a great God, and a great King above all gods. In His hand are the depths of the earth; the heights of the mountains are His also. The sea is His, for He made it, and His hands formed the dry land. (PSALM 95:3–5)

Did you see that? God's hand formed the dry land—the mountains, the hills, the valleys, the riverbeds. Yes, our God, Father, Son, and Holy Spirit, cares deeply about this world He created—and all the creatures who live on it. He is not leaving it for chance or for us to destroy but is controlling everything that happens for the good of His children—those who believe in Jesus Christ as Savior.

> Oh come, let us worship and bow down; let us kneel before the LORD, our Maker! For He is our God, and we are the people of His pasture, and the sheep of His hand. (PSALM 95:6–7)

Do you see how God still cares for the world He created? He holds it in His hand. He is the Good Shepherd who cares about every boy, girl, man, and woman who lives on earth. He holds us in His hand. He gave His Son, Jesus, to save us from sin, death, and the power of the devil. He saved us by His suffering and death on the cross and by His glorious resurrection to life on the third day.

When Jesus returns, He will transform this world, making it a perfect paradise for us to share with Him and one another for all eternity.

God's Covenant of Peace

READ EZEKIEL 34:25–30

When God brought Israel into the Promised Land, they enjoyed all that the land had to offer. But over time, they forgot about God and all He had given them. They set their hearts and minds on doing whatever they thought was right and trying to find things that made them happy. They never realized that a short life running away from God to chase after happiness ends in never-ending misery and suffering in hell.

Over and over, God sent messengers—prophets who warned His people they had turned away from God and needed to come back to Him. They needed to admit their sins and trust His promise to forgive them for the sake of His promised Son. But the Israelites ignored His prophets. God dried up the rains so they ran short of food. Israel came back to Him for a short time but turned away again when things got better.

Finally, God sent other nations to attack Israel and remind them how much they needed Him. But even when they turned back to God in their troubles, their repentance never lasted long. Once the trouble was gone, the Israelites became more evil than they had been before. They were even worse than the nations that didn't know about God. So the Lord allowed powerful nations to capture the Israelites and drag them from their homes to live in strange, far away places.

One of the Israelites who was taken away with many other Israelites was named Ezekiel. God chose him to be a prophet, a messenger who reminded the Israelites that God still cared about them. Ezekiel told the people about God's promise to bring them out of that distant nation and lead them back home.

For those who could remember living in the Promised Land, it didn't always seem like a good place to live. They remembered the dry spells, the lack of food, and the wild animals God had brought to turn His people from their sins. They weren't so sure they wanted to go back home. So Ezekiel gave them this promise from God:

> And I will make them and the places all around My hill a blessing, and I will send down the showers in their season; they shall be showers of blessing. And the trees of the field shall yield their fruit, and the earth shall yield its increase, and they shall be secure in their land. And they shall know that I am the LORD, when I break the bars of their yoke, and deliver them from the hand of those who enslaved them.
> (EZEKIEL 34:26–27)

That's the same thing Jesus did for us when He died on the cross. Because of our sin, we were prisoners of the devil, helpless to set ourselves free. But Jesus became human, came to earth, and suffered and died on the cross to set us free. Now He leads us from our prison of sin to the promised land of heaven, where we will live forever celebrating the love of God our Father and Jesus, our Savior.

God Continually Provides

READ LUKE 12:22–34

Living in this world can be hard and scary. We worry about so many things. Am I smart enough? Am I strong enough? Do people really like me? You may think things will be different when you grow up, but grown-ups worry the same way, just about different things. They worry if there will be enough money to last until they get paid again. They wonder if they will be able to keep their jobs. They worry about how they are going to be able to take care of their children and give them everything they need to grow up.

Those are things Adam and Eve never worried about while they were living in the Garden of Eden. They knew God was their loving Creator and that He would give them anything and everything they needed. That all changed when they decided they wanted to be free from God. The serpent told them that when they ate the fruit of the tree God had commanded them not to eat, they would become like God. But eating that fruit proved to them they were not God. Neither are we. So why do we worry about so many things as if there is no Creator God? Or as if we are God and have to do everything for ourselves?

Jesus, the Son of God, became human and was born for us at the first Christmas in Bethlehem. He grew up just like you and became a man. He always trusted His heavenly Father and didn't worry about anything. He knew God was watching over Him. So when God led Him out to the wilderness and told Him not to eat any food, Jesus didn't worry about going hungry. He prayed, looked to God, and went without food for forty days.

The devil came up to Jesus and said, "If You are the Son of God, command these stones to become loaves of bread" (Matthew 4:3). Have you ever tried to take a stone in your hand and command it to change into bread? Of course, we know that could never work for us. We are not God! But it could have worked for Jesus. He is the Son of God. But Jesus said, "It is written, 'Man shall not live by bread alone, but by every word that comes from the mouth of God'" (Matthew 4:4).

Jesus is God, but He didn't have to prove it to anyone. He patiently waited for His Father to take care of Him because He knew God loved Him. God loves you too. He loves you so much that He sent Jesus to the cross to suffer for your sins and the sins of all people to win a home with God in paradise.

As Jesus said, "Do not be anxious about your life" (Luke 12:22). God loves you and promises to give you everything you need as you pass through this wilderness, watching and waiting for Jesus to return.

The River of Life

READ REVELATION 22:1–5

The Books of Genesis and Revelation are perfect bookends to the Bible. The Bible starts with the Garden of Eden and ends with a new garden paradise, the new Jerusalem. The Garden of Eden is watered by four rivers, the new Jerusalem is watered by one—the river of life.

> Then the angel showed me the river of the water of life, bright as crystal, flowing from the throne of God and of the Lamb through the middle of the street of the city; also, on either side of the river, the tree of life with its twelve kinds of fruit, yielding its fruit each month. The leaves of the tree were for the healing of the nations. (REVELATION 22:1–2)

That tree of life was the whole reason Adam and Eve had to be driven out of the Garden of Eden when they sinned. Otherwise, they might have eaten from it and lived forever—cut off from God. That's another name for hell. God loved them too much for that. Eternal life in sin is no life at all—it is a never-ending death.

That is why Jesus took up another tree and carried it to Mount Calvary. It was a dead tree—the cross. But on that cross, life and death met, and life won. Jesus' blood transformed that dead tree into a new tree of life. When Jesus died, one of the Roman soldiers pierced His side with a spear to prove He was dead. And out of that wound gushed blood and water—the river of life.

We stepped into that river when we were baptized. Christ washed away all our sins, made us children of God, and filled us with His Spirit. Through His Word, He guides us through the wilderness of this earthly life. Sometimes it gets dry, and we get thirsty, but Jesus points us to the end of the road—and that river of life and tree of life waiting at the end. Read how John describes it:

> No longer will there be anything accursed, but the throne of God and of the Lamb will be in it, and His servants will worship Him. They will see His face, and His name will be on their foreheads. And night will be no more. They will need no light of lamp or sun, for the Lord God will be their light, and they will reign forever and ever. (REVELATION 22:3–5)

That is our future, sure and certain, solid as a rock, because we are covered in Jesus' grace.

Water from the Rock

Read Exodus 17:1–7. God sent Moses to free Israel from slavery in Egypt. But Pharaoh, king of Egypt, refused to let them go. God sent nine mighty plagues, giving Pharaoh the chance to obey his Creator after each, but Pharaoh stubbornly refused.

Finally, God's tenth plague killed all of the firstborn boys and men in Egypt, including Pharaoh's son. This time, Pharaoh did what God demanded and drove the Israelites out of his land. But then, after he thought about it, Pharaoh changed his mind and disobeyed God one more time. He sent his army to capture the Israelites and make them slaves again.

His army found Moses and Israel trapped against the Red Sea. But God sent a strong east wind to divide the water so Israel could pass through the sea on dry land. The Egyptian army charged in after them, but God stepped in. The army's chariot wheels clogged with mud, and they realized Israel's God was fighting against them. They turned to race back to where they started. But by this time, it was too late. God brought the water of the Red Sea down on top of them, drowning their entire army.

The people of Israel celebrated the great things God had done for them. After that, God led them into the wilderness to Mount Sinai, where God had first appeared to Moses in the burning bush. The wilderness was really, really dry. No crops or grass could grow there, so there was no food or water for the Israelites or their animals.

Israel was thirsty—and not very happy about this place where Moses had brought them. They complained that Moses brought them out of Egypt to kill them in the wilderness. God then told Moses to gather the people in front of a large rock. There God would stand before them. God commanded Moses to take his staff and strike the rock. When Moses did, water gushed out of the rock and provided water for every Israelite and their sheep, goats, and cattle.

What kind of rock was this? This week, we will look more closely at rocks and what they teach us about our God and Savior.

God Is the Rock

READ 2 SAMUEL 22:1–4

David was a young man who did great things, but not everyone was happy about it. He was too young to be a soldier when the giant Philistine soldier Goliath terrified King Saul and the Israelite army. But David killed the giant with a sling and a stone.

David joined Israel's army and fought to protect God's people from their enemies. God was with him. With God's help, David won many victories for King Saul and Israel.

But King Saul was a jealous king. He noticed people were singing songs about David, but they weren't singing about Saul. He got so worked up about it that Saul convinced himself David would soon try to kill him and steal his position as king. So Saul sent his whole army after David. Where in the world could David go to hide? David went up to the mountains of Israel and hid in caves.

Several times, Saul's men came close to capturing David. But each time, God protected him. David thought about it and realized that God was a lot like a rock—a strong place to hide when people were trying to hurt him. David wrote a song to praise God for saving him.

> The LORD is my rock and my fortress and my deliver, my God, my rock, in whom I take refuge, my shield, and the horn of my salvation, my stronghold and my refuge, my Savior; You save me from violence. I call upon the LORD, who is worthy to be praised, and I am saved from my enemies. (2 SAMUEL 22:2–4)

David learned to rely on God's protection. He wrote many psalms to share his thanks and praise to God and teach the people of God to pray to Him in times of trouble. David knew what it was like to have people judge him falsely, accuse him, and try to harm him.

Jesus also knew what it was like to be hated and to have people come after Him to destroy Him. But that did not stop Jesus from saying the things His heavenly Father wanted Him to say. Jesus taught people that they needed a Savior because of their sins—the wrong things they had thought, said, and done. Many weren't happy to hear about that, especially the priests and other Jewish leaders. They thought they were good people, not realizing that like all of Adam and Eve's children, they were sinners who needed God's Son, Jesus, to save them.

Finally, they convinced the Roman governor, Pontius Pilate, to put Jesus to death on a cross. But on that cross, Jesus was our rock, suffering the punishment we deserve for our sins. Since He rose on the third day and lives for us, He is always here to protect and guard us as we serve Him.

Fed by the Word

READ PSALM 1

Psalm 1 is a wonderful introduction to the Book of Psalms. It shows us two paths that stretch out in front of us. Will we walk with God in life or walk away from God? Wise people walk with God and are happy to read His Word, think about what He says, and talk about it day and night with other believers.

Psalm 1 gives us a picture to help us understand how important God's Word is for our lives:

> He is like a tree planted by streams of water that yields its fruit in its season, and its leaf does not wither. In all that he does, he prospers.
> (PSALM 1:3)

A believer who reads, studies, and thinks about the Bible is like a tree planted by a river. It will never dry up and has all the water it will ever need to grow fruit and stand tall and strong. That's what reading the Bible, talking about it in Bible study, and thinking about it day and night does for our spirit. It connects us to Jesus Christ, keeps us strong, and gives us power to do good works to help others and show them Jesus Christ. God's Word also fills us with hope and confidence no matter how hard our life gets.

But picture a tree or a plant in the middle of a field, far away from a river. If the rain stops falling for a long time, the leaves of that tree dry up, wither, and fall off. People who don't believe in Jesus and don't read the Bible are like those dried plants. When their lives get hard, they have no roots. They blow away in the wind.

The Bible is important because it is all about Jesus. It is God's Word to us, and it is made up of two great teachings: the Law and the Gospel. The Law shows us our sins and how we are helpless to save ourselves from God's punishment. But the Gospel shows us our Savior, Jesus Christ, God's Son, who became one of us and lived His life perfectly in our place. During His life, Jesus studied God's Word very carefully, talked about it, thought about it day and night, and taught it to others. When times got hard for Him, when people slapped Him, punched Him, spit on Him, and whipped Him, and during those six long hours when He was hanging on the cross, He held on tightly to God's Words and promises until His work was finished and each sin was paid completely.

The time you spend with Jesus reading your Bible is important because that is when He feeds you and satisfies your thirsty spirit!

The King and Princes

READ ISAIAH 32:1–8

Isaiah was a prophet to the Southern Kingdom of Judah about seven hundred years before Jesus was born. It was a time when some nations were growing very powerful and becoming empires. These empires built powerful armies. Little kingdoms like Israel and Judah were powerless to stand up against them. Only God could protect and keep them.

Isaiah wrote to warn the people of Judah to turn from their sins and believe in God's promises to send a Savior. In the Book of Isaiah, God revealed to His people many things about Jesus, the life He would live on earth, and His great mission. Isaiah wrote about how Jesus would be born of a virgin, His Baptism when God sent His Holy Spirit to Jesus, and Jesus' suffering and death and resurrection to life again.

In chapter 32, Isaiah describes the good things that will happen when Jesus reigns as King over His people:

> Behold, a king will reign in righteousness, and princes will rule in justice. Each will be like a hiding place from the wind, a shelter from the storm, like streams of water in a dry place, like the shade of a great rock in a weary land. (ISAIAH 32:1–2)

Jesus suffered for our sins on the cross, died, and was buried. Three days later, He rose from the dead and appeared to His followers. Forty days after that, He ascended or rose up into heaven and sat down on His throne at the right hand of God the Father Almighty. Jesus reigns as King over all of His creation.

He guards us like a shelter or hiding place. He satisfies all our needs and makes us grow and do good works the way streams of water bring life back to dry places. He stands like a great rock, throwing His cooling shade over us when our lives are hard and it feels like the sun is beating down on us.

Who are the princes? Those are the people Jesus raises up to share His reign. They include our parents, pastors, and teachers, and each of us who shares His story and fulfills the responsibilities God has for us.

Jesus Is Pierced

READ JOHN 19:31–36

This week's reading started with a large rock in the wilderness. The Israelites were thirsty and cried out to God, complaining that He wasn't taking care of them. God told Moses to take his staff and strike the rock. When Moses did, water came gushing out of the rock to satisfy Israel's thirst. There was also enough water for their flocks and herds.

Something similar happened after Jesus died on the cross. During those six long hours, God the Father turned His back on Jesus and punished Him for all of our sins—every single one. At the end of those six hours, Jesus shouted out in a loud voice, "It is finished!" (John 19:30). His work was complete, every single sin was paid in full, and God's anger at us was completely gone. Then Jesus breathed one last time and died.

A little later in the afternoon of that Good Friday, the sun was going down. The Jewish leaders asked Pontius Pilate to have his soldiers break the legs of the robbers next to Jesus so they would die and could be taken down from their crosses before the sun went down.

Jesus was crucified between the robbers. The soldiers broke the legs of both the robbers, but they knew Jesus was dead. Instead of breaking His legs, one of them grabbed a spear. John, one of His disciples who was there, wrote what the soldier did:

> But one of the soldiers pierced His side with a spear, and at once there came out blood and water. (JOHN 19:34)

That blood and water proved that Jesus had truly died. But more than that, it reminds us of that great rock that Moses struck when he was in the wilderness. The people and animals of Israel would have died there in the wilderness without water. You and I would have died in hell forever without Jesus dying for our sins. The water from His side reminds us of the water of our Baptism, where Jesus washed away our sins and made us God's children. The blood that poured from His side reminds us of Holy Communion, where Jesus gives His people His body and blood in bread and wine to eat and drink for forgiveness and strength.

Jesus Is the Rock

READ 1 CORINTHIANS 10:1–5

The second week closes with something the apostle Paul wrote in his First Letter to the Corinthians. Paul was warning the Christians living in the city of Corinth to turn from their sins and keep their eyes on Jesus. He told them about Israel's time in the wilderness to remind them and us how much we need God.

> For I do not want you to be unaware, brothers, that our fathers were all under the cloud, and all passed through the sea, and all were baptized into Moses in the cloud and in the sea, and all ate the same spiritual food, and all drank the same spiritual drink. For they drank from the spiritual Rock that followed them, and the Rock was Christ. (1 CORINTHIANS 10:1–4)

Paul isn't necessarily saying that the rock Moses struck in the wilderness was really Jesus. Paul wasn't necessarily saying that a big rock dragged itself along with the Israelites as they traveled through the wilderness. He was saying that there was no water inside that rock—certainly not rivers of water. He is teaching us that when Moses struck the rock with his staff, Jesus used His mighty power to make water pour out of it—just like the water and blood that flowed from His pierced side on the cross.

Jesus was with them all the way in their lives, and He is with you every place you will ever go. He will give you what you need throughout your life. He will protect you from harm and give you the strength to help other people when they are going through hard times in their lives.

He is not with us because we deserve Him. Just like the Israelites who grumbled and complained about the hard things that were happening to them and the scary wilderness around them, we are not always happy about the place God has put us in life. We may not like our teachers, brothers and sisters, classmates, or neighbors. But God loves us, and them. Since we are all sinners who could have died for our sins, Jesus came in our place.

Jesus lived the perfect life we can't live, and He suffered and died to take away the punishment that should have struck us.

Naaman Is Healed

Read 2 Kings 5:1–19. The story of Naaman is fascinating. He was a Gentile who learned of the God of Israel through his young servant who had been taken captive from Israel. Now stop and let that sink in a minute. This little girl was taken from her family and home against her will. She was a servant of the army commander whose people had attacked her city! But when she saw her master suffering from leprosy, she felt bad for him and made one comment that started a chain reaction of events:

> Would that my lord were with the prophet who is in Samaria! He would cure him of his leprosy. (2 KINGS 5:3)

Naaman had a real need—a need none of the false gods of Syria could heal. He told of this prophet to his king, who wrote a letter to the king of Israel, telling him to heal Naaman's leprosy.

The king of Israel was not a believer. He thought the king of Syria was setting a trap for him, looking for a reason to invade and start a war. But Elisha the prophet sent news to the king to send Naaman to him. Everyone would learn there is a true prophet in Israel, a prophet of the only true God in the heavens.

Naaman was reluctant, but when he obeyed the word of the Lord through the prophet and dipped himself in the waters of the Jordan River, he was healed.

This week, we will take a look at some other Bible passages that help us understand how God uses the water of Baptism to wash away our sins and make us His children.

Crossing over the Jordan

READ JOSHUA 4:1–6

God freed Israel from slavery in Egypt. Then He led them through the Red Sea, to Mount Sinai, and through the wilderness for forty years. When Moses died, God chose Joshua to lead His people into the Promised Land. But one huge barrier stood in their way—the Jordan River.

The Jordan always flows very fast, but the time God chose for Israel to cross the river was during the spring floods. The river was far deeper than normal, and flowing much more quickly. God commanded Joshua to tell the priests to carry the ark down to the riverbank, then step down in the river.

If a friend told you to step down into a flooded river, you'd be smart to run the other way. Without God's command, the Israelites would have watched the priests and the ark being swept downstream. But because of God's command, the minute they stepped into the water, the riverbed became dry ground beneath their feet. The river immediately stopped flowing, and the Israelites crossed over on dry ground. Joshua told the Israelites to make a memorial site using twelve stones out of the Jordan River. God commanded the people that when future generations would look at that memorial,

> Then you shall tell them that the waters of the Jordan were cut off before the ark of the covenant of the LORD. When it passed over the Jordan, the waters of the Jordan were cut off. So these stone shall be to the people of Israel a memorial forever. (JOSHUA 4:7)

God's Word and command made all the difference. The Lord Jesus commanded His followers to make disciples of all nations, baptizing them in the name of the Father and of the Son and of the Holy Spirit. By the power of that command, simple water poured over your head gave you a new birth, making you a child of God, washing away all of your sins, and filling you with the Holy Spirit. By the command of the Lord, the bread and wine on the altar are united with the true body and blood of Jesus Christ in Holy Communion. These give you all the benefits Jesus won for all of us in His innocent suffering and death on the cross—forgiveness for all of our sins, hope in eternal life for Jesus' sake, and the power to leave behind our lives of sin and live in faithful obedience to God.

When the Israelites looked at the memorial pile of stones, they remembered how God dried up the Jordan River at this very spot. When we look at the cross and empty tomb, we remember how Jesus opened the door of heaven for us and saved us from all our sins.

Cleansing of Sin

READ PSALM 51

Naaman the Syrian went down into the Jordan River, washed himself seven times in the river, and his leprosy was gone. Of course, the river water had no power in and of itself to cure leprosy, but the command of God met with faith—faith to go down and wash himself seven times. Actually, going down and washing himself those seven times in the Jordan gave Naaman a glimpse into the cleansing God was working in his body, healing him of his leprosy.

In the Bible, our sinfulness is often compared to leprosy. Leprosy is a disease that spreads and slowly attacks the body. Sin does the same to us, slowly spreading to every part of our life and attacking our heart, mind, body, and soul. Even great King David struggled with that.

David saw a beautiful married woman, and instead of obeying God's command to be satisfied with his own wives, David decided he wanted this woman for himself. When she got pregnant, he did everything he could think of to hide his sin. He even set her husband up to be killed in battle! He thought the people would think the baby was her dead husband's, and David would look like a hero when he married her.

But God knew what David had done. David's conscience filled him with great guilt. Finally, God sent a prophet, who told David of his sin. Then David wrote the words of Psalm 51:

> Have mercy on me, O God, according to Your steadfast love; according to
> Your abundant mercy blot out my transgressions. Wash me thoroughly
> from my iniquity, and cleanse me from my sin! (PSALM 51:1-2)

David knew no matter what soap he used, no matter how hot the water was, he could never wash away his own sins. Only God could do that. But that is why Jesus poured out His blood on the cross. Jesus suffered and died in David's place—and in your place—so that God could forgive the sins we commit against Him and other people.

Jesus cleanses us in water. Not hot bath water, but in the water of Baptism, which receives its power from His Word of command that He speaks over that baptismal water. Baptism washes away all of our sins and makes us clean forever.

Fountain of Cleansing in Jesus

READ ZECHARIAH 12:10–13:1

Zechariah was one of the last prophets of the Old Testament. God gave him an important job. This included teaching the people of Israel many things about the last week before Jesus' death, especially how Jesus would save us from our sins. In chapters 12–13, Zechariah makes a surprising prediction of something we talked about last week:

> And I will pour out on the house of David and the inhabitants of Jerusalem a spirit of grace and pleas for mercy, so that, when they look on Me, on Him whom they have pierced, they shall mourn for Him, as one mourns for an only child, and weep bitterly over Him, as one weeps a firstborn. . . . On that day there shall be a fountain opened for the house of David and the inhabitants of Jerusalem, to cleanse them from sin and uncleanness. (ZECHARIAH 12:10; 13:1)

Last week, you read about the soldier who pierced Jesus' side with a spear to make sure He was dead. While Jesus' dead body was hanging on the cross, the soldier pierced Jesus' side, and water and blood came pouring out. Five hundred years before Jesus was born, Zechariah wrote about that piercing and described it as a fountain opened to cleanse us from sin and uncleanness.

The Church Year is divided into many different seasons, and the season of Lent is one of those long seasons where we talk about the reasons Jesus died and confess our sins. Lent is a season to stop and look closely at the cross of Jesus. There we realize just how serious our sins are—how much they hurt other people and how much they hurt and anger God. That is God's one and only Son hanging on that cross. He suffered for our sins, giving His life breath, pouring out His precious blood, praying for God to forgive us because we do not know what we are doing.

And when it was all finished, what happened? God opened up a fountain through the spear that pierced Jesus' side. That fountain washes away all your sins in the water of Baptism, and in the body and blood of Jesus Christ in Holy Communion.

But the Lamb did not stay dead. On the third day, Jesus rose from the dead to promise that death will not keep hold of us or our loved ones because Jesus has given all believers the promise of eternal life.

Jesus Is Baptized

READ MATTHEW 3:13–17

Jesus' Baptism is one of the strangest things when you stop to think about it. It makes no sense! And it made no sense to John the Baptist either. When Jesus came to John to be baptized, John told Jesus,

> I need to be baptized by You, and do You come to me? (MATTHEW 3:14)

It was the right question for John to ask Jesus. Baptism is to wash the sins away from sinners. Why in the world does Jesus, the spotless, sinless Son of God, need to be baptized? Could you imagine having to take another bath when you were just in there, washing carefully and thoroughly?

But there was a side of Baptism John was not seeing. Jesus answered,

> Let it be so now, for thus it is fitting for us to fulfill all righteousness.
> (MATTHEW 3:15)

That's when John understood God planned to join all sinners with their Savior, Jesus. They would bring their sins to the Baptism water, and Jesus would pick up those sins and carry them to the cross. So John agreed to baptize Jesus. God the Father spoke His approval: "This is My beloved Son, with whom I am well pleased" (Matthew 3:17). The Holy Spirit descended like a dove and landed on Him.

In the Gospel of John, John the Baptist pointed to Jesus after His Baptism and said, "Behold, the Lamb of God, who takes away the sin of the world!" (John 1:29).

We sinners come to the water of Baptism filthy with sin and leave it spotless and pure. Jesus comes to Baptism spotless and sinless. He leaves carrying the sin of the world. He carried that sin clear to Calvary, where He paid the price of its punishment as He hung on the cross. Jesus' Baptism made the waters of Baptism clean forever, connecting us to Jesus' death and resurrection. Paul describes the connection between Jesus' Baptism and our Baptism this way:

> Do you not know that all of us who have been baptized into Christ Jesus were baptized into His death? We were buried therefore with Him by baptism into death, in order that, just as Christ was raised from the dead by the glory of the Father, we too might walk in newness of life.
> (ROMANS 6:3–4)

Jesus' Baptism and His death and resurrection gives our Baptism the power to wash away all of our sins.

Washed in the Name of Jesus

READ 1 CORINTHIANS 6:9–11

The apostle Paul wrote about the amazing washing of our Baptism in the name of Jesus Christ and the power of the Holy Spirit. He first says, "Or do you not know that the unrighteous will not inherit the kingdom of God?" (1 Corinthians 6:9). Then he lists some really bad things people do to one another.

Are you on that list? We may not do really bad sins like killing people, stealing things, or starting fires, but all of us are unrighteous too. We hurt other people with our unkind words and mean actions. So are we too bad to inherit the kingdom of God? Are we too bad to live with God forever when Jesus Christ returns and fixes His broken creation?

Paul tells us, "And such were some of you" (1 Corinthians 6:11). Some of the members in the Church in Corinth had done some really bad things. So did Paul kick them out of the Church because their sins were too bad? No. He wrote,

> **And such were some of you. But you were washed, you were sanctified, you were justified in the name of the Lord Jesus Christ and by the Spirit of our God.** (1 CORINTHIANS 6:11)

Let's look at those three phrases very carefully.

"You were washed." Paul is talking about Baptism. They were baptized, and the power of God's Word in the water washed away their sins.

"You were sanctified." To sanctify means to make someone holy so they do good things that please God.

"You were justified." To justify means to make someone acceptable to God. Or, to use Paul's word from the start of this reading, through Baptism, Jesus makes a person right, able to inherit the kingdom of God. How? Because in Baptism, God has taken away all of your sins and given you Jesus' perfect life. Because of Jesus' death on the cross, your sins are gone, and you are ready to live with God forever.

Jesus at the Well

Read John 4:1–30. Our next "water" Bible reading took place at a well in Samaria. Jesus was traveling north from Jerusalem to Galilee through the region of Samaria. Samaritans and Jews had a long, troubled history. Let's just say they really hated each other. About midday, Jesus and the disciples reached a Samaritan village. Jesus was so tired and thirsty that He couldn't keep walking. So Jesus sat down by a well to rest. Meanwhile, He sent His disciples into the village to buy food for them to eat.

While He waited for them to return, a Samaritan woman walked toward the well to draw water. Jesus said, "Give Me a drink" (John 4:7). The woman was shocked. Men didn't usually talk to women they didn't know, especially a Jewish man and a Samaritan woman. The Jews hated the Samaritans.

Jesus used that water to change the discussion and talk about "living water"—the forgiveness, peace, and salvation He had come into the world to bring to all people. Water was the perfect way to introduce the topic and help her understand how much she needed to be right with God.

The woman's spirit was thirsty for God's love, peace, and forgiveness. She needed to know God cared about her. Jesus started with the idea that drinking water can satisfy our body's thirst, refresh our physical strength, and give our bodies energy to keep moving. Then He taught her that our spirit works the same way as our body. Physical water cannot satisfy our spirit. Our spirit needs to be filled with "living water," the Holy Spirit, who brings us Jesus' Word and His promise of forgiveness and peace.

This week, we will take a look at some other Bible passages that help us understand this living water that alone can satisfy our spiritual thirst.

A Well in the Desert

READ NUMBERS 21:16–20

Let's start this week at a different well. The reading for today talks about the days of Moses when he was leading the Israelites after their exodus from Egypt. The journey continued in the dry, frightening wilderness.

Normally, when you read an account describing God giving water to the Israelites, it starts with the Israelites being thirsty and grumbling and griping that Moses brought Israel out of Egypt to kill them all in the wilderness with thirst. But this time, God was the one who mentioned water first. He told Moses,

> Gather the people together, so that I may give them water. (NUMBERS 21:16)

Notice that God did not bring water from a rock this time. Instead, Israel believed God. They were so confident God would give them water that they began singing a joyful song:

> Spring up, O well!—Sing to it!—the well that the princes made, that the nobles of the people dug, with the scepter and with their staffs.
> (NUMBERS 21:17–18)

It was a song of faith and confidence that God would keep His promise. Moses gathered the people, the Israelite leaders started digging with the rods and sticks they used while walking, and water sprang up from below the surface.

God knows us. He always provides the things we need, often before we realize how much we need them. But it is wonderful when we know we can trust that God is watching over us, ready to provide the things we need. God was preparing them as they trusted God's promise and watched their leaders dig. He was training them for the days when they would come to the Promised Land and see the huge walls of the Canaanite nations. Instead of being filled with fear and worry, as they had been when ten spies gave a bad report of the land in Numbers 13, they were learning to trust God—to stand back confidently and watch Him take care of their needs.

When we think of Jesus coming to save us, we see how God provides for all our needs. Our greatest need of all is to be right with God. If we are not in a right relationship with God when this life ends, we will be separated from God forever, spending all eternity thirsting for God's presence, which we will never have. But God made us right through Jesus. Jesus took our sins and guilt on His own shoulders and carried them to the cross. There He suffered God's punishment in our place so we can go free. He rose again on the third day, assuring us that He will raise us from the dead and we will live in His presence forever, singing His praises.

God gave His very best treasure for us—His own Son—so we can be confident God will keep His promises to give us everything we need for this life too.

The Soul Thirsts for God

READ PSALM 42

Today, we jump ahead to a psalm that teaches us about our soul's thirst by comparing it to a thirsty deer:

> As a deer pants for flowing streams, so pants my soul for You, O God. My soul thirsts for God, for the living God. When shall I come and appear before God? (PSALM 42:1–2)

What an amazing picture! Can you imagine a thirsty deer standing under the blazing sun, panting as it looks all around for a stream to drink from? It climbs up one hill, then another, and sees no stream, just more hills ahead.

That is what our spirit feels like when we aren't going to church to hear God's Word or when we aren't reading the Bible or devotions at home. We can try a lot of different, fun-sounding things to satisfy the empty spot deep down in our souls, but that is a space only God can fill.

Jesus knew that feeling. He knew what it was like when His body was dried out and aching for a drink. When He was hanging on the cross, suffering for our sins, He said, "I thirst" (John 19:28).

But even more, Jesus knew the pain of a really thirsty soul. Because the heavenly Father was punishing Jesus for our sins, He turned His back on Jesus. The Son of God cried out in a loud voice, "My God, My God, why have You forsaken Me?" (MATTHEW 27:46).

Because Jesus was punished for our sins, He won forgiveness for every one of those sins. We are at peace with God, who is always with us, satisfying our spirits with His living water. For Jesus' sake, we never need to worry about being alone.

God, the Fountain of Living Waters

READ JEREMIAH 2:9–13

Spiritual thirst is a huge problem. When Adam and Eve disobeyed God, they were cut off from the only One who can satisfy our thirsty spirits. When we were conceived, we inherited their sinful nature. With that sinful nature, our spirits also inherited a deep hunger and thirst that only God can satisfy. But our sinful nature makes us think we're thirsty only for worldly things. If only we had more money, more friends, and more likes on social media. If we were stronger, faster, or smarter, then this deep thirst inside would go away.

That was the problem God's people had in the Old Testament. God brought them out of Egypt, led them through the wilderness, and brought them into the Promised Land. He taught them the right way to come into His presence and receive the living water their spirits needed. He gave them priests to teach them their sins, teach them how God forgave them when they made sacrifices that pointed ahead to Jesus' great sacrifice on the cross, and promised them that God was leading them to an even greater day when they would see Him face-to-face and live with Him forever.

But His people did something hard to imagine. They turned away from God. Then they ran after the false gods of the nations that God had driven out before them. It made no sense. Not one of those false gods had been able to stand against Israel's true God, but now Israel was turning to those false gods. The prophet Jeremiah explained it very clearly:

> For My people have committed two evils: they have forsaken Me, the fountain of living waters, and hewed out cisterns for themselves, broken cisterns that can hold no water. (JEREMIAH 2:13)

A cistern is a large tank that people dig (or hew) to catch and hold rainwater. Imagine having a spring of clean, delicious water running near your house but digging out a dirty cistern that leaks and can't hold the rainwater. It sounds ridiculous, but it's something we do often.

When we feel scared, lonely, or insecure, instead of opening the Bible and reading God's promises, we turn to social media to see what people think about our latest post. We turn to people who can be so mean, cruel, and wrong in their ideas and thoughts.

Jesus never trusted Himself to what other people said or thought about Him. He only cared about what God His heavenly Father said. He studied God's Word and memorized it so that He could always remember what God thought. He prayed constantly. Even when He was suffering for our sins on the cross, Jesus kept praying to His Father, refusing to turn to someone or something else to help Him.

Jesus covers you with His grace. He loved you enough to leave His home in heaven and live in this sad world. He carried your sins to the cross and suffered terribly for you because He loves you so much. He is the stream of living water that will keep your soul healthy, strong, filled with joy, and satisfied all your life.

Rivers of Living Water

Read John 7:37–39

Jesus used the idea of thirst to describe how our spirits need to be connected to God for us to be able to live. He was in Jerusalem in the temple courts teaching.

> On the last day of the feast, the great day, Jesus stood up and cried out, "If anyone thirsts, let him come to Me and drink. Whoever believes in Me, as the Scripture has said, 'Out of his heart will flow rivers of living water.'" Now this He said about the Spirit, whom those who believed in Him were to receive. (John 7:37–39)

Jesus wasn't handing out bottles of water in the temple. He was talking to people whose spirits were thirsting for a close relationship to God. He spoke to people who really needed to know how much God loves them, how He sent His Son to pay the penalty for their sins in His death on the cross.

Think about how amazing that time was. If you felt sad, depressed, worried, or hopeless, Jesus was right there. All you had to do was look in His face to see how much He loves you and how much He wants you to know that He will never leave you or turn against you.

Of course, Jesus died, rose again, and ascended into heaven. He promised to be with us always, but we can't see His face, hear His voice in our ears, or touch Him with our hands. But He has given each believer His Holy Spirit. When you were baptized, Jesus washed away your sins, God the Father claimed you as His own son or daughter, and the Holy Spirit came to live inside you and make your heart, mind, soul, and body His own temple—the place where He lives in the world. He created your faith and keeps it strong as you read the Bible, come to God's house to worship, and receive His body and blood in Holy Communion when you are confirmed.

With the Holy Spirit in the heart of each believer, we all have that living water flowing in us and out to others. Through our actions, we can show others how much God loves them and cares about them. Through our words, we can share the water of life as we talk about how Jesus died and rose again to save all people.

Springs of Living Water

READ REVELATION 7:13–17

The theme of living water carries all the way to the last book of the Bible, Revelation. In chapter 7, we see the saints in heaven—the spirits of believing men, women, and children who died trusting Jesus as their one and only Savior. They are gathered around the throne of God, praising Him for His endless love and the salvation Jesus won for them and all of us. John tells us about these people and what God is still doing for them while they are waiting for Judgment Day. On that wonderful day, Jesus will raise their bodies and they will live with Him and all of us believers in the new heavens and the new earth.

> Then one of the elders addressed me, saying, "Who are these, clothed in white robes, and from where have they come?" I said to him, "Sir, you know." And he said to me, "These are the ones coming out of the great tribulation. They have washed their robes and made them white in the blood of the Lamb. Therefore they are before the throne of God, and serve Him day and night in His temple; and He who sits on the throne will shelter them with His presence. They shall hunger no more, neither thirst anymore; the sun shall not strike them, nor any scorching heat. For the Lamb in the midst of the throne will be their shepherd, and He will guide them to springs of living water, and God will wipe away every tear from their eyes." (REVELATION 7:13–17)

God is giving you a peek into your future, and what a marvelous future it is! After we die—or on the day Jesus returns, if that happens before we die—we will be changed and transformed. All our sins and our sinful nature will be taken away from us forever, and we will be holy and perfect. All the saints around us will be perfect too. No more jealousy, mistrust, pain, tears, or suffering. We will be with God, bathed in the glorious light that shines from His beautiful face.

We will live in a new paradise even more wonderful than the Garden of Eden. God will feed us and satisfy our thirst—body, heart, mind, and soul. And we will delight to live with God and drink of His living water forever.

Jesus Washes the Disciples' Feet

Read John 13:1–20. This week, we will consider a precious moment during Jesus' Last Supper the night before He died on the cross to save us from our sins. His disciples were in the Upper Room, arguing about which of them would be considered the greatest by later generations. Jesus didn't stop their argument; He didn't yell at them or embarrass them. He silently rose from the cushion on which He was lying, took off His outer garment, wrapped a towel around His waist, and then went around the table, washing the disciples' feet, one by one.

It was a staggering moment to see the mighty Son of God kneeling down and washing their feet—a task usually done by the lowest servant in a household. Without a word, Jesus showed the Twelve that Christians don't spend their time trying to figure out how to impress people so we can get more "likes." We spend our time focused on the people around us in our homes, schools, neighborhoods, and teams. We listen to learn what they need. We ask God to show us ways we can show them how much God loves them, how much we love them, and how we can show how important they are to God.

This week, we will take a look at some other Bible passages that show us how Jesus Christ put our needs before His, suffering and dying to save us. By looking at Him, we learn how to put other people's needs before our own. Because of Jesus, God our Father is always watching over us and taking care of all of our needs.

Love Your Neighbor as Yourself

READ LEVITICUS 19:9–18

We start the readings for this week at Mount Sinai, halfway between Egypt and the Promised Land. God had led Moses and the people of Israel to Sinai to reveal His glory to them and teach them how they were to live as His people in the world. He gave them His Ten Commandments and told Moses to come to the top of Sinai. There, for forty days, God told Moses to teach His people how they were to worship Him and how they were to live together, taking care of one another and making everyone else's lives better.

He talked about how they could help their poor neighbors, the widows who had lost their husbands, and the children who had lost their parents.

> When you reap the harvest of your land, you shall not reap your field right up to its edge, neither shall you gather the gleanings after your harvest. And you shall not strip your vineyard bare, neither shall you gather the fallen grapes of your vineyard. You shall leave them for the poor and for the sojourner: I am the LORD your God. You shall not steal; you shall not deal falsely; you shall not lie to one another. . . . You shall not take vengeance or bear a grudge against the sons of your own people, but you shall love your neighbor as yourself: I am the LORD. (LEVITICUS 19:9–11, 18)

Israel was mainly a farming country. People lived off the food they grew on their land. God was directing them to leave some behind when they harvested their crops so that needy neighbors could go into their fields, gardens, and vineyards and have food. God ended His instruction by saying words Jesus often said: "You shall love your neighbor as yourself." What would you want your neighbor to do for you if you ended up losing your parents? Or if you were too old, injured, or sick to grow your own food? You would want them to help you. So now we can do the same for them.

That is exactly what Jesus did during His life on earth. He silently stood up from His throne in heaven, set aside His power and glory as the Son of God, and came down to this world. He put on a human body and took care of needy people around Him. He fed the hungry, healed the sick, gave sight to those who were blind, and gave hearing to those who were deaf. From Jesus, we learn to love our neighbors when we take care of their needs.

But Jesus knew the people around Him had a far greater need. They were sinners who were cut off from God because of their sins. They needed to know God's love and forgiveness. So He went around teaching people about His Father's love. He went to the cross to take away God's anger at our sins and win God's peace and forgiveness through His death. He rose again to show us that He will raise us to live forever too.

You and I do well when we take care of the needs of our friends, family, and neighbors. But we do much better when we share God's love and forgiveness as we tell them the story of Jesus' life, death, and resurrection.

God's Care for the Needy

Read Psalm 9

David knew what it was to be needy. After he killed the giant Goliath, he joined the army of King Saul and fought hard to protect God's people, Israel. God gave him many victories. King Saul became very jealous of David's success and was afraid David would kill him to steal his throne. Saul sent his army to kill David, forcing David to go into hiding and live in caves.

During this time in his life, David wrote Psalm 9 to remind us God watches over each of us. He knows when other people mistreat us. God loves us as His own children. David wrote,

> The Lord is a stronghold for the oppressed, a stronghold in times of trouble. And those who know Your name put their trust in You, for You, O Lord, have not forsaken those who seek You. Sing praises to the Lord, who sits enthroned in Zion! Tell among the peoples His deeds! For He who avenges blood is mindful of them; He does not forget the cry of the afflicted. Be gracious to me, O Lord! See my affliction from those who hate me, O You who lift me up from the gates of death. . . . For the needy shall not always be forgotten, and the hope of the poor shall not perish forever. (Psalm 9:9–13, 18)

Sometimes, other people mistreat us, whether it's kids at school or bullies on the internet. They make us miserable. Even though we pray and pray about it, nothing seems to change. Psalm 9 reminds us that God knows, remembers, and will do something about it.

Think of the twelve disciples in that Upper Room. During the Last Supper, Jesus kept telling them over and over that He was going to die the next day, but three days later, He would rise again. They didn't hear the resurrection part, probably because hearing about the dying part hurt them so much.

Jesus rose from the table and washed their feet. He knew the same powerful enemies that wanted to kill Him hated His followers too. The worst of those enemies was the devil. He tempts us to sin. Then, when we break God's Law and do things we shouldn't do, he tells us God could never love or forgive us after what we have done.

Jesus washed the disciples' feet to show them He loved them, even though He knew Judas would betray Him, Peter would deny ever knowing Him, and the others would turn and run away from Him to save themselves. He went to the cross the next day to show He loved them all the way to a bitter death. By that suffering, He took away the anger God felt against them for their sins.

Jesus loves you the exact same way. In Holy Baptism, He washed away all your sins. In His Word, He assures you that He has loved you from the very beginning—even before He formed the heavens and the earth. He came to live in this world, to die on the cross, and to rise to life again to save you from your sins. And He is coming again on the Last Day to take you home forever.

That love sets us free from our enemies and gives us the strength to love the people around us, care about them, and share what Jesus did to save them.

The Suffering Servant

READ ISAIAH 53:1–12

Out of all the books written by the prophets in the Old Testament, none teaches us more about Jesus' great mission to save us than Isaiah. In chapter 53, Isaiah writes a powerful description of Jesus suffering on the cross, explaining clearly that Jesus was suffering the punishment we deserve for our sins. He was condemned, crucified, and killed so we could be freed from God's wrath and live forever with Him—our Lord, Savior, and God.

> Surely He has borne our griefs and carried our sorrows; yet we esteemed Him stricken, smitten by God, and afflicted. But He was pierced for our transgressions; He was crushed for our iniquities; upon Him was the chastisement that brought us peace, and with His wounds we are healed. All we like sheep have gone astray; we have turned—every one— to his own way; and the LORD has laid on Him the iniquity of us all.
>
> (ISAIAH 53:4–6)

Did you notice the great exchange that fills these verses? Jesus bears or carries our griefs; He carries our sorrows. He was pierced for our transgressions, crushed for our iniquities. To chastise someone means to punish that person, especially with a whip. Jesus suffered the whipping that gave us peace. His wounds heal us. We have all gone astray from God's Law the way sheep wander off in different directions. We all deserve God's punishment here on earth and forever in hell. But our sins and our punishment were laid on Jesus. And our Savior, Jesus, bore them willingly because He loves us so much.

The night before Good Friday, Jesus took off His outer garment and got down on His hands and knees to wash His disciples' feet. This showed His disciples how much He loved them. That demonstration was something they would never forget. The next day, He picked up the cross, although He was already carrying our heavy sins. When He carried it to Calvary with the help of a stranger named Simon, He stretched out His hands to be nailed to the cross and was hung between heaven and earth.

The world has never seen such injustice, but Jesus suffered it all because of His deep love for God His Father and for all of us lost children of Adam and Eve. He was thinking of each of us when He cried out, "Father, forgive them, for they know not what they do" (Luke 23:34).

Maybe you have been hurt by hard words someone said or felt the sting of being mistreated by people you thought were your friends. Go to Jesus' cross to learn God's love and forgiveness and receive the power to forgive those who sin against you. When you do this and follow Jesus' example, it's like you will be getting down on your hands and knees to wash their feet too.

Servant of All

READ MATTHEW 20:26–28

The Last Supper was not the first time the disciples had argued about which of them was the greatest. The same argument arose when Jesus was leading His disciples up to Jerusalem for His final Passover. There He would die on the cross to save us from our sins.

The disciples sensed that a huge moment was going to happen at this Passover. They probably thought Jesus would go to the temple and become the earthly king over Israel. If He would drive out the Roman armies, the people of Israel would be free. And, of course, they thought Jesus would not forget His faithful Twelve. They thought He would place them in high positions to rule in His kingdom. Their minds were puffed up with dreams of power and glory. That got them looking at one another, arguing about which of them would be considered the greatest. Before silently washing their feet, Jesus taught them how it would be in His kingdom:

> It shall not be so among you. But whoever would be great among you must be your servant, and whoever would be first among you must be your slave, even as the Son of Man came not to be served but to serve, and to give His life as a ransom for many. (MATTHEW 20:26–28)

Now think of Jesus washing their feet. Jesus, the great and powerful Son of God, was not too proud to drop down onto His hands and knees to wash their dirty, smelly feet. He was not too high and mighty to be arrested, tied up, slapped, punched, and spat upon. The mighty King of kings let Himself be whipped, crowned with thorns, and nailed to the cross.

Indeed, Jesus had not come to be served by His human creatures but to serve each of us by giving His life as the ransom to buy us back from sin, death, and hell.

Looking at Jesus serving us changes things, doesn't it? Suddenly, being the star in the school play or the hero of the basketball team isn't quite as important. What is more important is seeing that hurting classmate that no one else notices or the kid being bullied with no one to help. Smiling at him, sitting together at lunch, joining him on the playground, and standing up for her on social media become important ways of following Jesus' example. As we care for others, we share how Jesus Christ loves them and sacrificed Himself to save them forever.

God's Yes in Christ

READ 2 CORINTHIANS 1:12–21

Jesus died on the cross, then rose again the third day. Forty days later, He ascended or rose up into heaven and rules all creation at His Father's right hand. Paul wrote to the Corinthians about the day Jesus will come back to earth to judge the world:

> For our boast is this, the testimony of our conscience, that we behaved in the world with simplicity and godly sincerity, not by earthly wisdom but by the grace of God, and supremely so toward you. For we are not writing to you anything other than what you read and understand and I hope you will fully understand—just as you did partially understand us—that on the day of our Lord Jesus you will boast of us as we will boast of you. (2 CORINTHIANS 1:12–14)

When Paul talks about "the day of our Lord Jesus," he means Judgment Day. On that day, Jesus will raise all the dead, and we will all stand before Him to be judged. Paul says on that great day that the Corinthians will boast about Paul and his fellow missionaries, and Paul will boast about the Corinthians. Isn't that incredible?

If you ask people what they will say when they stand before Jesus' judgment seat on the Last Day, many say they will tell him about the good things they did during their lives. We are all tempted to think that way sometimes. But that is boasting about ourselves. Paul shows us that is not what true believers will do. We will point to other Christians, boast about the good things they did, and they will boast about us.

True believers know we deserve to be found guilty by Jesus and locked into hell forever. The good works we believers do are only possible because Jesus has taken away our sins by His suffering and death on the cross and made us children of God. The Holy Spirit came to us through the Gospel and Baptism, created faith in us, and kept that faith strong. He gave us the power and the desire to look out for others and show them God's love.

Every boast we could possibly make on Judgment Day starts with Jesus Christ, the Son of God who loves us and gave Himself for us. Paul continues,

> The Son of God, Jesus Christ, whom we proclaimed among you, Silvanus and Timothy and I, was not Yes and No, but in Him it is always Yes. For all the promises of God find their Yes in Him. That is why it is through Him that we utter our Amen to God for His glory. And it is God who establishes us with you in Christ, and has anointed us. (2 CORINTHIANS 1:19–21)

God keeps all His promises to us because of Jesus Christ and only because of Jesus. That's why God made His promises for Jesus' sake. And that is why we pray in Jesus' name with all of our prayers. When we ask for forgiveness, God's help out of trouble, or for God to save us, we ask it for Jesus' sake—never for our own sakes. And since we ask in Jesus' name and for Jesus' sake in our prayers, we can be absolutely sure that God will do what He promised. When Christ returns to judge the world, He will welcome us to our eternal home in His presence—the home of God, our heavenly Father.

Thousands Believe in Jesus

Read Acts 2:1–41. Fifty days after Jesus rose from the dead, and ten days after He ascended into heaven and took His throne at God the Father's right hand, Jesus poured out His Holy Spirit like living water upon His Church.

The twelve disciples were gathered on Pentecost in Jerusalem. Suddenly, a loud sound like a mighty rushing wind came from heaven and filled the house where they were. Divided tongues, which looked like they were made of fire, appeared to them and rested on each of them. They were filled with the Holy Spirit and began sharing the Good News of Jesus Christ with all the people gathered together in Jerusalem. Many Jews were gathered together at the time to celebrate the great Old Testament harvest festival called Pentecost. Streams of living water flowed out of each apostle, pouring out to all the thirsty souls gathered around them. That day, the Holy Spirit brought three thousand people to believe in Jesus Christ and be baptized by the apostles.

Since that day, the Word of God has gone forth from believers by the power of the Holy Spirit like streams of water in a dry and thirsty desert. This week, we will take a look at some other Bible passages that show us this was God's desire in all ages to save the lost children of Adam and Eve through Holy Spirit-created faith in His Son, Jesus Christ.

49

That the World May Know

Read 1 Kings 8:41–43

Israel's great King David had one huge dream. He was thankful for God's love and protection while he was hiding from King Saul. He was also thankful for all the ways God helped him when he became king over Israel. He wanted to show his thanks by building a fabulous house, a temple, that would reveal God's great and awesome glory. Through it, David thought, God would show His greatness to each Israelite as well as to strangers from foreign countries who learned of God's goodness and were brought to faith by the Holy Spirit.

But David was a soldier. He had been in many battles, fighting to protect God's people, Israel, to save them from all their enemies. God wanted His temple to be built in a reign of peace to show the world He was a God who delighted in peace and safety. He chose David's son Solomon as the one who would build the temple. David gathered supplies for the temple and gave Solomon careful directions for building the temple.

Solomon did all that his father, David, told him to do. He built the temple and gathered all Israel together to dedicate it to the glory of God. Part of the dedication was a prayer in which Solomon asked God to be merciful to the people of Israel when they sinned and call them back to God to confess their sins, turn from them, and receive God's forgiveness. The sacrifices God's people made assured them of God's forgiveness and pointed ahead to the one great sacrifice the promised Savior would make for all people of all time on the cross.

But Solomon also thought of people outside the nation of Israel. He prayed for the Gentiles, the nations of the world, and other children of Adam and Eve that God loved as much as His people Israel:

> Likewise, when a foreigner, who is not of Your people Israel, comes from a far country for Your name's sake (for they shall hear of Your great name and Your mighty hand, and of Your outstretched arm), when he comes and prays toward this house, hear in heaven Your dwelling place and do according to all for which the foreigner calls to You, in order that all the peoples of the earth may know Your name and fear You, as do Your people Israel, and that they may know that this house that I have built is called by Your name. (1 Kings 8:41–43)

King Solomon understood that when God made a nation from the children of Abraham and called them His own possession, it was not because God was rejecting all the other nations of the world. He raised up Israel so that through the good deeds He did for Israel, every nation could know that the God of Israel was the only true God. As the others saw God's power in Israel, they would turn from their false gods to trust in the true God alone and find salvation in the Savior God promised to raise from His people, Israel.

God loves us Christians. He has made us His own children for Jesus' sake. But God loves every descendant of Adam and Eve. He loves every man, woman, and child He has created. It doesn't matter where they live on earth, what language they speak, or what nation they belong to. God loves them all.

Jesus, His Son, shared that love for all. He took all the sins of all people on Himself and won salvation for everyone through His suffering and death on the cross. Before He ascended into heaven, He commanded His disciples to bring the Gospel to all the corners of the world and make disciples of every nation. He began that mission and empowered His apostles and His Church to do that by pouring His Holy Spirit out on Pentecost. He gave you His Holy Spirit at your Baptism so that you may share the Good News of Jesus in your home, with your friends, fellow students, teammates, and everywhere you go throughout your life. His Holy Spirit, the living waters, will flow to others through the loving things you do and the story of Jesus you share.

Declare God's Glory

READ PSALM 96

God's plan of salvation was very clear to the people who lived in the time of the Old Testament, even hundreds of years before Jesus was born. Psalm 96 speaks of God's love for all people. It recalls Israel's mission to tell of God's great works so that people from every nation might turn from their false gods and trust in the true God of Israel, and His promised Savior, Jesus Christ. Some of the verses in Psalm 96 remind Israel of the mission God has for them:

> Sing to the LORD, bless His name; tell of His salvation from day to day. Declare His glory among the nations, His marvelous works among all the peoples! For great is the LORD, and greatly to be praised; He is to be feared above all gods. For all the gods of the peoples are worthless idols, but the LORD made the heavens. (PSALM 96:2–5)

In his Small Catechism, Martin Luther talks about what it means to have a false god. A god is anything we fear, love, or trust more than we fear, love, and trust in God, our Father, and our Savior, Jesus Christ. A good way to know if we are treating someone or something in our life like a god is to ask, Would I be willing to give it up or lose it if God asked me to? Would you be willing to give up your favorite sport, video game, or social media account?

God rarely asks us to choose like that, but just thinking about it can help us see clearly if we have made something a god or not. That's when it is time to stop and think about what our God did for us. He loved us so much that He sent His Son, Jesus, into our lost and fallen world, giving Him into the hands of people who hated Him, beat Him, and killed Him on a cross. Do any of the people or things we love in this world love us like God loves us?

Jesus suffered and died for our sins on the cross. He rose from the dead. Forty days later, He ascended or rose up into heaven and took His place at the right hand of God the Father. Jesus received all power and authority in heaven and on earth. He reigns over every galaxy, star, and planet in space and every kingdom and nation on earth. No person or thing can stop Him from carrying out God the Father's plan. On Judgment Day, Jesus will raise the dead, judge the nations, and restore His creation shattered by sin. The psalm continues with what we are to tell the people around us,

> Say among the nations, "The LORD reigns! Yes, the world is established; it shall never be moved; He will judge the peoples with equity." Let the heavens be glad, and let the earth rejoice; let the sea roar, and all that fills it; let the field exult, and everything in it! Then shall all the trees of the forest sing for joy before the LORD, for He comes, for He comes to judge the earth. He will judge the world in righteousness, and the peoples in His faithfulness. (PSALM 96:10–13)

Jesus is coming again, and all of creation waits for that day when death will die and life will reign under God's hand. Then He will restore each of His believers and His creation perfectly.

God's Desire That All Be Saved

READ EZEKIEL 33:10–16

The prophet Ezekiel lived and preached in a really tough time. He was among the people of the Southern Kingdom of Judah, which fell to the Babylonian army. Along with the king and a great number of people, Ezekiel was dragged off from his homeland to live in a strange place. He saw the suffering of war, starvation, and disease. Yet God raised him up because of His great concern for Ezekiel and all the exiles living in sorrow. The people of Israel realized they had turned away from God and were suffering what they deserved. They thought God had given up on them, that He would never bring them home, and that they would die in their sins. Here is the message God gave Ezekiel to assure His people:

> And you, son of man, say to the house of Israel, Thus have you said: "Surely our transgressions and our sins are upon us, and we rot away because of them. How then can we live?" Say to them, As I live, declares the Lord GOD, I have no pleasure in the death of the wicked, but that the wicked turn from his way and live; turn back, turn back from your evil ways, for why will you die, O house of Israel? (EZEKIEL 33:10–11)

The devil wanted the people of Judah to believe their sins were so great that God could not possibly love them and want to forgive them. The devil tempted them to believe the lie that they had given up any chance to be the people of God.

But God wanted them to know the truth. God never delights to see someone die in unbelief. No one is too far away, too filthy a sinner, for God to say, "I won't forgive you." That is why He sent Jesus to the cross, carrying every single sin of Adam and Eve and of each of us. He has paid for every sin. What God wants, more than anything, is for all people to believe in Jesus and enjoy eternal life with Him in heaven.

That is where each believer in the entire Christian Church comes in. We are God's messengers, like Ezekiel. He sends us out to people who are suffering for their sins and feel they are too far gone for God to love them. By showing them our love even when they have treated us badly, we show them their God and Creator still loves them. When we tell them the great price Jesus Christ paid to save them, the Spirit pours that living water across their dry souls. As Jesus said, there is great rejoicing and celebration in heaven over every single sinner who repents and trusts in Jesus' great salvation.

Jesus Is the Way

READ JOHN 14:1–6

The night before Jesus died, He gathered His disciples together for one last meal. He told them He was leaving them and that they could not follow Him right away. But He assured them later they would be with Him. He was talking about His death and burial. But even more, He was talking about His ascension into heaven. For a time, they would not see Him any longer, but when their life and its work was over, they would be reunited with Him forever.

But the disciples did not understand. All they could focus on was losing Jesus, and their hearts were deeply upset. So Jesus told them,

> Let not your hearts be troubled. Believe in God; believe also in Me. In My Father's house are many rooms. If it were not so, would I have told you that I go to prepare a place for you? And if I go and prepare a place for you, I will come again and will take you to Myself, that where I am you may be also. And you know the way to where I am going. (JOHN 14:1–4)

That is such a beautiful picture. Jesus is the groom; His Church, the Bride. In this beautiful picture, Jesus married the Church through His death and resurrection. He would leave for a brief time to prepare a place where we can share eternal life together with Him in God's house.

Notice that Jesus said His Father's house has many rooms, not just a few. There is room for the three thousand who believed on Pentecost. There is room for millions of believers who have lived and died since that day and for all believers between now and Christ's return. There is room for you as well. But Thomas was still confused.

> Thomas said to him, "Lord, we do not know where You are going. How can we know the way?" Jesus said to him, "I am the way, and the truth, and the life. No one comes to the Father except through Me. (JOHN 14:5–6)

That was such a reassuring thing for Jesus to say. Many people think the path to God the Father is through the things we say and do—a special kind of life that earns God's congratulations and a welcome into heaven. But that is just a dead end. How can we ever know if we are on the right path, that we have done enough or lived a life that is good enough?

That is the sad uncertainty that people of other religions constantly face. Muslims, Jews, Mormons, and Buddhists always have to wonder if they have done enough or are good enough. Jesus takes away that fear, dread, and uncertainty. He is the way to the Father. Jesus has done it all. He lived the perfect life of obedience to the Father that none of us can. He took our guilt and sin upon Himself and satisfied God's justice by suffering the punishment we deserve.

That is the assurance we can give to people around us who want to go to heaven but aren't sure how to get there.

Proclaiming Christ

READ 1 PETER 4:7–11

The apostle Peter wrote many things about the end of the world and the coming of Jesus Christ to judge the living and the dead whose bodies have been raised alive again. In his first letter, he gives us instruction on how to live as we wait excitedly for Jesus to return to us:

> The end of all things is at hand; therefore be self-controlled and sober-minded for the sake of your prayers. Above all, keep loving one another earnestly, since love covers a multitude of sins. Show hospitality to one another without grumbling. As each has received a gift, use it to serve one another, as good stewards of God's varied grace: whoever speaks, as one who speaks oracles of God; whoever serves, as one who serves by the strength that God supplies—in order that in everything God may be glorified through Jesus Christ. To Him belong glory and dominion forever and ever. Amen. (1 PETER 4:7–11)

Peter teaches us to remember that Jesus could return at any time, so we watch for Him and pray for Him to make and keep us ready for that great day. He reminds us to love one another from the heart, because love "covers a multitude of sins" (v. 8). That doesn't mean we try to cover up sins and hide them from God. It means we forgive people who sin against us and cover up their sins from others. We don't post their sins on social media and gossip about them to all of our friends. We keep it between God and us and protect their reputation. That makes them love us more when we forgive their sins and treat them kindly.

We use the gifts God has given us to help one another remember God's love in Jesus more clearly. For some, that means speaking the "oracles of God" (v. 11). Oracles are the things God has said to us in the Bible. So we tell others what the Bible teaches about our Savior, Jesus Christ, and His great sacrifice on the cross to save us from our sins. Sometimes it means serving other people, especially those who need help from us.

Whether we speak or serve, it all comes from God and turns our eyes back to God. We don't take credit for the things we do or say. We give God the credit in Jesus, our Savior. Our God alone deserves the credit, praise, and recognition for all the good things that exist.

Lydia Hears God's Word

Read Acts 16:11–15, 40. Our final week looks at water in a different way. The story revolves around a woman named Lydia who first heard the Good News of Jesus from the apostles while she was sitting beside a river. She heard the Good News of Jesus and believed.

Lydia sold purple clothing and fabric. In those days, the dye to make clothes purple was very rare and cost a lot of money. So only people with a lot of money could afford it. Lydia had a nice home, and she opened her house to Paul and the believers in Philippi as a place to worship God while the number of believers was growing.

When Paul and his friend Silas were mistreated by the people of Philippi and put in prison, God sent an earthquake, which gave Paul the chance to share Jesus' story with the jailer. After Paul and Silas were released, Lydia met them and sent them on their way to the next town.

This week, we will take a look at some other Bible passages that speak about God's Word, which shows us Jesus, our Savior, and the love of God our Father.

The Joy of God's Word

READ NEHEMIAH 8:9–12

Last week, we read about Ezekiel, a prophet for the people of Judah. God allowed the Israelites to be taken into captivity in Babylon because they had turned away from Him, worshiped false gods, and mistreated their neighbors. When the temple was destroyed, the people realized how terribly they had treated God. They knew they deserved to be punished and were afraid God would never forgive them and take them back home. Through Ezekiel, the Lord promised to bring His people back to the land of Israel. He also promised to send the Savior He had first promised to Adam and Eve after they ate the forbidden fruit in the Garden of Eden.

Seventy years after Judah was taken captive, God gave Babylon to a nation named Persia. He led the king of Persia to permit the exiles to return to rebuild Solomon's temple in Jerusalem. The exiles rebuilt the temple, repaired the walls around Jerusalem, then gathered to thank God for keeping His promise to bring them home and for helping them succeed. As they gathered, the Word of God was read to the people.

> And Nehemiah, who was the governor, and Ezra the priest and scribe, and the Levites who taught the people said to all the people, "This day is holy to the LORD your God; do not mourn or weep." For all the people wept as they heard the words of the Law. Then he said to them, "Go your way. Eat the fat and drink sweet wine and send portions to anyone who has nothing ready, for this day is holy to our Lord. And do not be grieved, for the joy of the LORD is your strength." So the Levites calmed all the people, saying, "Be quiet, for this day is holy; do not be grieved." And all the people went their way to eat and drink and to send portions and to make great rejoicing, because they had understood the words that were declared to them. (NEHEMIAH 8:9–12)

God's Word teaches us Law and Gospel. The Law shows us our sin and warns us of the punishment we deserve because we have disobeyed God. When the exiles returned and heard the Law, they felt horrible for what they had done, and they cried in their guilt.

We also should feel guilty when God's Word reveals our sins. The Law of God shows us our sins and makes us afraid of being punished by God. But God doesn't want us to stay in our guilt, crying and feeling bad about ourselves forever.

The Good News, or the Gospel, is that in Jesus, God forgives us our sins. He wraps us in His arms, wipes the tears from our eyes, and tells us to look at the Good News of His love shown in His dear Son, our Lord and Savior, Jesus Christ. Yes, we have done horrible things, and we deserve to be punished by God. But Jesus stepped forward and took that punishment in our place. He took our sins and guilt on Himself and died on the cross to satisfy God's wrath and make things right between God and us.

God doesn't want us to live with crushing guilt, hating ourselves because of the horrible things we have said or done. He wants us to turn our eyes to Jesus, our Savior, and rejoice that because He lives, we, too, will live forever with Him in our heavenly Father's house.

Meditating on God's Word

READ PSALM 119:9–16

The Psalms talk about the importance and beauty of God's Word. Psalm 119, the longest psalm, teaches us all about the Bible and how important it is for our lives.

> How can a young man keep his way pure? By guarding it according to Your word. With my whole heart I seek You; let me not wander from Your commandments! I have stored up Your word in my heart, that I might not sin against You. Blessed are You, O LORD; teach me Your statutes! With my lips I declare all the rules of Your mouth. In the way of Your testimonies I delight as much as in all riches. I will meditate on Your precepts and fix my eyes on Your ways. I will delight in Your statutes; I will not forget Your word. (PSALM 119:9–16)

God loves us very much. He wants us to know His love, and He keeps us safe from the things that could destroy our faith, make our lives miserable, and make us spend eternity separated from Him in hell. So He gave us His Bible, with its Law to show us our sin and its Gospel to show us our Savior.

Psalm 119 reflects Jesus' attitude toward God's Word. We are to learn it, memorize it, and meditate on it like He did. It is especially important in our youth. There are so many voices in the world trying to give you advice, encouraging you to focus on yourself, your feelings, your desires, and the things that sound exciting to you, especially the things God knows will hurt you.

God gives us boundaries through His Commandments to protect us from things that would destroy our faith and keep us from having an impact in our world when we follow Him. God doesn't want us living lives of hurt, regret, and guilt. The best way to do that is to let God's Word guide and inform us.

But even when we sin by crossing the lines God has set before us, blow up relationships, and destroy opportunities, Christ is there to forgive and restore us. He paid the price for each time we cross God's line into sin, and He won peace for us through His suffering and death. And even if we destroy a relationship or lose out on an opportunity because of our sins, He has the power to give us new brothers and sisters in His Church and open doors we never expected. When the Last Day comes and our life reaches its end, Jesus will be there to bring us to a glorious everlasting life!

The Power of God's Word

READ ISAIAH 55:1–13

Today, we will look at a special invitation from the prophet Isaiah. He has told us about Jesus' life, including His death and resurrection (see Isaiah 53). Now, two chapters later, he shares the New Testament invitation of Jesus Christ, which will continue to ring out through the Church until Christ returns:

> Come, everyone who thirsts, come to the waters; and he who has no money come, buy and eat! Come, buy wine and milk without money and without price. Why do you spend your money for that which is not bread, and your labor for that which does not satisfy? Listen diligently to me, and eat what is good, and delight yourselves in rich food. (ISAIAH 55:1–2)

The world doesn't offer anything for free. Even free gaming apps come at a cost—either watching an ad (which makes money for the app developers) or slowly progressing through the game until you finally cave in and pay for upgrades to keep up with other players.

But Jesus offers us something more meaningful and satisfying than any video game or entertainment. He offers us forgiveness, peace with God, a life of meaning and impact, and an eternity enjoying God's awesome presence in the amazing new heavens and the new earth.

It is absolutely free of charge because Jesus Christ paid the full price for you and every person. There are no requirements you have to meet. Jesus met them all already during His earthly life when He perfectly obeyed God's will and demands. There is no punishment for our sins and failures because Jesus already paid the punishment when He suffered and died on the cross for us.

But this offer of forgiveness, peace, hope, joy, and eternal life is a limited-time offer.

> Seek the LORD while He may be found; call upon Him while He is near; let the wicked forsake his way, and the unrighteous man his thoughts; let him return to the LORD, that He may have compassion on him, and to our God, for He will abundantly pardon. For My thoughts are not your thoughts, neither are your ways My ways, declares the LORD. For as the heavens are higher than the earth, so are My ways higher than your ways and My thoughts than your thoughts. (ISAIAH 55:6–9)

Right now is the time to seek and find the Lord Jesus. Many people put off turning to Jesus. They wait until sometime in the future. A lot of young people get confirmed then drop out of the church during high school and college, intending to come back when they are grown. But that's a dangerous game to play. Drift away from God's Word and Sacraments for a few years, and your soul will dry up without that living water. Many who walk away from receiving God's gifts of Word and Sacrament for a short time never come back to receive that living water.

Yes, during your life on this earth, Jesus Christ is near, calling out to you. But when this life ends, you won't be able to find Him, and He will not answer your call. It will be too late. The end of life seems very far away, or like it will never come, but it surely will. And you never know when. Young people die of illnesses, car accidents, and other causes often. But even if that doesn't happen to you, you never know when Christ will return. Today is the day to read God's Word and have your faith formed by the Holy Spirit. This weekend is the time to go to church, receive God's gifts through Word and Sacrament, and be fed by the living water that satisfies your soul. God promises it will:

> For as the rain and the snow come down from heaven and do not return there but water the earth, making it bring forth and sprout, giving seed to the sower and bread to the eater, so shall My word be that goes out from My mouth; it shall not return to Me empty, but it shall accomplish that which I purpose, and shall succeed in the thing for which I sent it.
> (Isaiah 55:10–11)

Treasuring God's Word

READ MATTHEW 6:19–24

As we have already read, Jesus loved and treasured God's Word. We know that by the time He was twelve years old, He had studied and learned the writings of the Bible and was able to ask deep questions and answer hard questions from the Jewish priests and teachers.

You might think, well, of course. Jesus was God! Though that is true, Jesus set aside His divine powers when He was conceived. He did not open up His divine memory like a computer hard drive. He took the same time to read and learn of all the things He could have taken His time to learn and study, and He knew that God's Word was the most important for this life and the next.

He taught His followers not to be distracted by working to gain earthly things like money, popularity, or possessions:

> Do not lay up for yourselves treasures on earth, where moth and rust destroy and where thieves break in and steal, but lay up for yourselves treasures in heaven, where neither moth nor rust destroys and where thieves do not break in and steal. For where your treasure is, there your heart will be also. (MATTHEW 6:19–21)

It may seem like people who are rich and have a lot of friends have it all. But they don't. Earthly treasures can be stolen, lost, or taken away. Jesus offers us something so much better. He offers us a magnificent home in the new heavens and the new earth where we will be able to celebrate and live with our God and Savior forever.

The funny thing about it is if you want earthly treasures, you're going to have to work hard to gain them. If you want to be popular, you will likely have to act like you are someone you are not, try to hide your sinfulness, and pretend you are funny, perfect, and smart all the time. But when it comes to gaining treasures in heaven, you don't have to do anything. Jesus already did it all for you. He earned your way to heaven by His perfect life. He took your sin and guilt. He suffered God's punishment for your sins Himself and suffered on the cross so you won't have to suffer forever in hell.

That's probably the final reason Jesus warned us to store up treasures in heaven instead of storing up treasures on earth. What if you spend all your life with your back turned toward God because you are doing everything you can to get as much money as you can, have more followers on social media than anyone who has gone before you, and own the biggest house, car, and yacht in the world? What if you get all of those things but end up turning away from Jesus and losing your faith? What happens when this short life is over, and you are standing before Jesus' judgment seat? None of the things you did on earth will save you, and the great treasures of heaven will be gone forever.

Jesus was right. Put God first, drink deeply of the living water of His Word and Sacraments, then you will be satisfied with your life on earth and can look forward to the never-ending wonders of heaven!

Equipped with God's Word

READ 2 TIMOTHY 3:14–17

This book comes to a close with some words the apostle Paul wrote to a young pastor and travel companion, Timothy. For every pastor and every Christian, the one thing that is the most important is for us to keep believing in Jesus Christ. If we lose this faith, we lose everything. That can be kind of scary when you are looking at all the changes happening in the world around us, and all the unknown paths our lives will take in the coming years. *Will I still believe in Jesus when I'm in my 30s?*

The Bible has really good news for us. Faith doesn't come from us. It isn't something you have to make or dig up from deep inside. Faith is a gift God gives you. It is something the Holy Spirit creates in you through the Gospel and Holy Baptism. And it isn't even up to you or me to keep that faith strong inside. That is also the Holy Spirit's job. It's like a tree God plants by a river. As long as water is flowing in that river, that tree will grow stronger and stronger. The living water the Holy Spirit uses to make our faith grow stronger and stronger is the Bible and Holy Communion. As Paul tells Timothy, keep reading and studying the Bible on your own, in church, and with others!

> But as for you, continue in what you have learned and have firmly believed, knowing from whom you learned it and how from childhood you have been acquainted with the sacred writings, which are able to make you wise for salvation through faith in Christ Jesus. All Scripture is breathed out by God and profitable for teaching, for reproof, for correction, and for training in righteousness, that the man of God may be complete, equipped for every good work. (2 TIMOTHY 3:14–17)

When Timothy was a child, his mother and grandmother taught him the faith. When he was a little boy, he learned the Bible, which teaches us about God's plan to save us from our sin. He heard and read God's promises to the people in the Old Testament to send His Son to save them. He also heard and read God's promises in the New Testament about how Jesus came from heaven, lived His earthly life, suffered and died to take away our sin and guilt, and how He rose again.

What is so special about the Bible? God the Holy Spirit gave every single word to the people who wrote it. It shows us our sin, then points us to Jesus and how He saved us from that sin. When you read the Bible, you can trust every single thing you read because all of it is true. And it all fits together as it talks about Jesus and how He saved us.

May God the Holy Spirit keep you close to Jesus and keep your faith strong as you read and hear the Good News in the Bible. May God always satisfy your spirit with the living water from heaven.